SHATTERED MY TRUTH MY SCARS MY RISE

Shattered My Truth My Scars My Rise

QUANSHEEBA LONG

Contents

SHATTERED. MY TRUTH MY SCARS MY RISE

Cover by Quansheeba Long
Cover Image by Quentin Long/ QCK Photography

ISBN: 979-8-218-67120-4 (Paperbook)

First Printing, 2025

Dedication

This book is dedicated to my Mother Wanda who has shown me strength that has helped me become the strong woman I am.

In addition, I dedicate this book to my Auntie Sharon. She has stood with me in some of the most difficult moments in my life. She has prayed for me through and has always been there for me no matter what. These two women have been my inspiration as a mother and woman of God.

Lastly, but surely not least, I dedicate this book to my husband Quentin who has shown me love that I never knew existed and has held my hand in the darkest hour I've experienced in my life bringing light, love and kindness. I love you baby and thank you for everything.
With you by my side I've been reclaimed.

Psalm 37 "Delight yourself also in the Lord, and He shall give you the desires of your heart"

Forward

This is not just a book. This is a battle cry wrapped in grace. This is for the girl who was too young to know that manipulation isn't love.

For the woman who stayed longer than she should have because she believed loyalty meant pain.

 For the survivor who doesn't look like what she's been through but feels every echo of it when she's alone. This story is not filtered. It is not watered down. It is not made pretty to be palatable. It is the truth and it is sacred.

   This book tells you:

   You can be groomed, abused, and still be powerful. - Loyalty should never cost you your soul.

You don't have to look like what you've been through. - You can survive what was meant to kill you.

   Healing is messy, but worth it. God still sends love after the pain.
Your voice is a weapon and your truth is enough.

If you've ever felt scared, silenced, or shattered this is your mirror, your map, your moment. Because once you choose yourself, everything changes.

And Queen, I promise you this:

Your scars are not shame—they are proof that you fought back.
You are not what he did to you.

You are who you are becoming.

Quentin S. Long

Preface

I didn't write this book to expose anyone. I wrote it to free myself and to reach the woman still trapped in a story she didn't ask to be in.

For years, I carried pain that was dressed in silence. I hid emotional and physical bruises beneath my strength, cried in secret, and convinced myself that staying was a form of love and loyalty.

I was young, loyal, scared... and yet, somehow, still full of hope.

I hope that my life will change.

Hope that I'd survive.

Hope that God would rescue me from the cycle I couldn't name but deeply felt.

This book is for the woman who's been called crazy for crying. For the woman who's been told, "just pray about it," while she's breaking inside. For the woman who's smiling in public and shattering in private. For the woman who wonders if she's still worth saving. You are. I was and Still Am!

This is my truth. It's not sugarcoated, watered down, or filtered to make anyone comfortable. Because healing doesn't come from hiding.

Healing comes when you look at your scars and say, "This didn't kill me. And it won't define me." I pray that in these pages, you find your voice again.

I pray you find validation, healing, fire, and freedom.

Most of all, I pray you remember who you are.

You are not broken.

You are not what they did.

You are God's daughter.

You are rising.

Welcome to my story. Now let's write your new beginning together.

Quansheeba L. Long

Introduction

This book is more than a story, it's a safe space. A mirror. A healing guide. A hand to hold when your own feels too weak to keep reaching.

Shattered: My Truth. My Scars. My Rise. is written for every woman and young girl who's endured what others will never understand.

Each chapter is a piece of my truth, but also a reflection of what so many survivors have lived through abuse, manipulation, heartbreak, shame, silence, and ultimately... survival.

You'll find fifteen raw, unfiltered chapters, each paired with:

A focus scripture to center your spirit
A journal prompt to help you reflect and reclaim your voice
A powerful affirmation to declare over your life

These chapters are meant to be felt not just read. You don't have to rush. You don't have to perform. Just breathe. Be honest. Cry if you need to. Shout if you must.
Let this book meet you exactly where you are.

Some of the things you'll read may stir up old memories.

Some may make you angry.

Some may set you free.

And all of it is valid.

Use this book however your soul needs:

Read it all in one night—or one page at a time

Come back to the affirmations daily

Share it with a sister who still in the storm.

There is no wrong way to heal—only the courage it takes to begin.

So, start here. Start now.

This time, let your story work for you not against you.

You're not just surviving anymore.

You're Rising!

Chapter 1

Childhood Trauma

I was only a child.

Not a woman. Not an object. Just a little girl, lying on a bed in a cousin's house, pretending to be asleep.

But even pretending couldn't protect me.

Somehow, in his drunken mind, that man thought it was okay to come into that room—into *my* space—and do the unthinkable. He didn't just violate my body. He didn't just cross a line. He stole something from me that night that I didn't even know could be taken: my soul.

He snatched my innocence in the silence.

He walked out whole, while I lay there shattered.

I never screamed. I didn't know how.

I froze. I disappeared inside myself.

When my mother came to pick me up from being at the club that night, the music and laughter still clung to her like perfume. I remember the way the door creaked open, the sound of her keys dropping on the counter, and how my heart thundered in my chest like a silent scream waiting to be heard. I had been holding it in for what felt like hours, afraid, ashamed, confused—but the moment I saw her, everything I had bottled up came crashing out.

I cried.

No, I wept.

The kind of cry that comes from the gut, from a place too deep for words to reach.

All I could say through the sobs was, "Mama, he hurt me. I need you. I need you to protect me."

I can still see the way her body stiffened. The joy from her night out evaporated in an instant. Her eyes—usually warm and tired—turned sharp with rage. She didn't ask me if I was sure. She didn't make excuses. She didn't tell me to be quiet. She believed me. Right away.

There was a fire in her spirit I had never seen before. I remember her pacing, grabbing her purse, yelling for someone to take her to where he was. She was ready to go to war for me—and that changed everything. I wasn't just a little girl in pain anymore. I was a daughter worth defending.

From that night forward, she never let me out of her sight. I became her shadow. She kept me glued to her hip, and in her presence, I felt safe again. I'd curl into her arms at night, still shaking from what happened, and she'd stroke my hair and hum the old songs she used to sing when I was a baby. Her lap became my sanctuary. Her scent, my safety. Her anger, my armor.

She made sure I didn't return to that house. She kept watch over my every move. When I was afraid to sleep, she stayed awake with me. When I questioned my worth, she spoke life over me. For a while, I felt like maybe the nightmare was over. Maybe with her by my side, I could start to believe that I was okay. That I was clean. That I was whole.

She became my safe place. The first home I had after the one inside me was broken.

Her love couldn't undo what happened, but it made survival possible. It made breathing easier. It gave me hope.

But as time passed, life didn't stop throwing punches. Bills piled up. Relationships strained. Trust frayed. And though my mama loved me, she was still human. Still hurting. Still carrying her own weight.

Until one day...

Even my safe place started to slip away.

* * *

F ocus Scripture: Psalm 34:18 *"The Lord is close to the brokenhearted and saves those who are crushed in spirit."*

Journal Prompt:

Reflect on the version of yourself that experienced trauma as a child. What did she need in those moments? What was she missing that you can now give her as an adult? Write down how you will care for her now—from a place of power, healing, and self-love.

Affirmation:

My childhood may have been marked by pain, but it will not define my future. I am not the trauma I endured—I am the healing I am walking in. I choose to nurture the inner child within me. I am safe. I am loved. I am whole.

Chapter 2

The Love I Never Got

Trauma.
Misunderstanding.
Sexual abuse.
They didn't just visit my life—they unpacked their bags and stayed.

There were so many things I was afraid to say out loud, because I knew it would destroy family lines. I held those secrets in my bones, and the weight of them started to show. I'd break out in hives along my back. I'd cry in silence. I'd rebel loudly. And the more I acted out, the more my mama cried—and the more I longed for her to just *see me* and hold me close.

But instead of reaching for me, she pulled away.
She turned her heart from me.
She started focusing on her own life.
And it crushed me.

I felt abandoned. Not enough. A burden. And that broke something in me that never quite healed—not even now. I tried to make her see me. I wanted her to love me like she loved my sister. But instead, I became the reflection of something she couldn't face. Maybe I reminded her of a part of herself. Maybe

I was her mirror. All I know is that her love became cold, her discipline became harsh, and her arms stopped being safe.

And while she was looking away, *it* happened again.

This time, it was a close family member. Another secret I had to swallow. I stayed close to the abuser—not because I liked it, but because my mind was so twisted by trauma I didn't know what safety even looked like anymore. If I told, everything would blow up. Who would believe me? So I buried it. I acted out. I lost control. But no one ever asked *why*. They just called me wild.

We used to be a strong, united family.
Then we broke.
And no one knew why I was falling apart.

The only place I thought I felt pure love from my mom was this one moment: she had just met her new boyfriend, and I stayed over his house with her and she taught me how to make french toast. I held onto that moment like it was life itself. I made French toast over and over—trying to taste that memory, trying to relive her warmth. But it never tasted the same again.

At twelve, I left her house and swore I'd never come back. It was too painful. I learned how to run away from my problems and never face them
At fourteen, we moved to a new city for a "fresh start."
But by then, I was already too numb. Too lost. I didn't want a new life—I wanted the pain to stop.

I used sex to cope, just to feel something. Just to feel *seen*.
And when an older woman came into my life and showed me attention, I clung to her—not because I was attracted to her, but because I was starving for love. Starving for connection. Starving for someone to just want me and not hurt me.

That didn't last.
More trauma came.
I ended up moving to North Carolina to live with my sister, and I thought that would finally be the fresh start I needed. But I

didn't know her heart was broken too. She was dealing with her own demons, and so was I. Neither of us were whole enough to hold the other.

And that's when the darkness truly deepened.

I was exposed to a life I had no business being in.

Men—grown men—looked at me with intentions no child should ever encounter.

They said things that still echo in my mind, and tried things I can barely whisper.

Looking back now, I shake my head in shame and pain. They were grown. I was a child.

And in all of this...

That's what led me straight into the arms of *him*.

The man I thought would finally love and protect me.

The man I thought would make me feel safe again.

But he wasn't safety. He was another storm.

* * *

Focus Scripture: Romans 8:38-39 For I am convinced that neither death nor life, neither angels nor demons, neither the present nor the future, nor any powers... will be able to separate us from the love of God that is in Christ Jesus our Lord."

Journal Prompt:

Write a letter to your younger self—at age 12, 14, or even that little girl making french toast. Tell her what she deserved to hear. Tell her she was never the problem. Tell her how you now understand the pain she carried and how you are choosing to love and protect her today. Let this letter be your way of reclaiming her story.

Affirmation: I am not the sum of what others did to me. I was never a burden. I was a little girl needing love, not punishment. Today, I affirm that I am worthy of peace, worthy of safety, and worthy of love that doesn't hurt. God is healing every part of me—from the confused child to the rebellious teen to the woman learning to rise.

Chapter 3

When Innocence Was Tested Again

It's hard to explain what happens when abuse doesn't stop at one moment, one person, or one place. After that first night when my innocence was stolen, it felt like abuse had found my address. It followed me. It knew my name.

I had a childhood friend I loved dearly. We would laugh, play outside for hours, and dream up little-girl adventures like the world couldn't touch us. She was older, a little wiser, someone I trusted with my whole heart. But one day, the game changed. We were playing—just playing—and then she touched me.

And I felt a fire in my body I didn't understand.

It wasn't love.

It wasn't comfort.

It was confusion.

The kind of confusion that digs deep into your soul and makes you question everything. I didn't like girls. I didn't *want* that. But my body was reacting in ways my mind couldn't process, and all I could do was freeze again. Why would she do this to me? Why didn't she protect me like I thought she would? Why couldn't she just be my friend?

I felt betrayed. Violated. Ashamed.

And underneath it all—I felt scared.

Because this wasn't the man from before.

This was someone I trusted.

This was a girl.

This was different.

The spirit of confusion tried to wrap itself around my identity. It tried to tangle my understanding of what love was, what friendship meant, and who I was becoming. And for years, I carried that moment like a secret wound—one I didn't know how to name.

But now, as a grown woman, I see it clearer. I see the brokenness in her too. I see the signs I missed—the way she held pain in her eyes even when she smiled, the way she needed control because she had none in her own life. I don't excuse it. I still hurt. I still carry the scar.

But I pray for her now.

Because I know someone touched her too.

The cycle tried to repeat itself through her hands.

And I was just the next little girl in its path.

But God.

God has been untangling those lies.

Restoring the places where shame once lived.

Reclaiming my story with grace and truth.

I am not what happened to me.

I am not what someone else projected onto me.

I am a woman of worth.

And confusion does not get the final say.

God does.

* * *

Focus Scripture: Isaiah 61:3 "...to bestow on them a crown of beauty instead of ashes, the oil of joy instead of mourning, and a garment of praise instead of a spirit of despair. They will be called oaks of righteousness, a planting of the Lord for the display of his splendor."

Journal Prompt:
Think about a moment from your childhood or youth that left you feeling confused, silenced, or ashamed. What would you say to the little girl inside you now? Write her a letter of love, protection, and truth. Let her know what she deserved then—and what she still deserves now.

Affirmation: What happened to me does not define me. I am not confused—I am called. I am not broken—I am becoming. My body is not shameful. My story is sacred. I honor my truth and release what was never mine to carry.

Chapter 4

The Meet Up

It was spring—March to be exact—and I was living with my aunt at the time. That day, I was walking to the park—the spot where everybody showed up when the weather turned warm. Nice cars, basketball games, music in the air. It was where you went to be seen.

As I passed one house, my home girl called out to me: "Yo, this dude wanna holla at you!"

I laughed. "Who?"

She pointed behind her. "My homeboy."

And there he was. Clean. Cool. Driving an '88 Oldsmobile. And me? I was already in a bad space emotionally. So his confidence, the way he carried himself—it felt like escape. I liked men who were a little hard, who had money, who could provide what I never had. And he seemed like he could.

We exchanged numbers. At first, he was just another name in my phone.

But then he called. And he kept calling. He was charming. I told him about me. He gave just enough of himself to keep me interested. I braided his hair. He gave me gifts. Slipped money in my pocket. Made me feel seen. Wanted. Before I realized it, I was hooked.

But what I didn't know was that I was being led into something I wasn't ready for—and something I didn't deserve.

I was just fifteen when my life changed forever. It didn't start with a bruise or a scream. It started on a highway—with a man too old for me and a heart too young to know better. He saw my innocence as an invitation not to love me, but to mold me. He called it love, but it was never that. He wanted control, not companionship.

He wanted submission, not support. He told me how to dress. Who I could talk to. What dreams I should let die. I didn't see it then—I thought he was protecting me. I thought love meant sacrifice. I thought being chosen meant surrendering myself.

But I wasn't being loved. I was being groomed. When the abuse started, it didn't always show on my skin. It came in the form of silence, confusion, and fear. I lost my voice. I lost my light. I lost myself trying to be enough for a man who only wanted to own me. But even in the darkest moments, I held on to something sacred: hope. A flicker. A whisper.

A part of me that knew deep down:

This isn't love. Love doesn't suffocate. Love doesn't silence. Love doesn't destroy.

This book? It isn't just for me.

It's for the girl I used to be.

It's for the woman still trapped in a story she never asked for.

It's for the survivor still learning to call it abuse.

I'm telling my truth because I survived.

And if you're reading this,

I want you to know you can survive too.

* * *

Focus Scripture: Psalm 23:4 *"Even though I walk through the valley of the shadow of death, I will fear no evil, for you are with me."*

Journal Prompt: What part of your story have you been afraid to tell, and why? Write one truth you've been holding back.

Affirmation: My voice is powerful. My truth deserves to be heard.

Chapter 5

When Abuse Doesn't Look Like Abuse

By the time I met him—the one who would silence my spirit and twist my world—I had already been trained to endure pain. His words weren't new. His control wasn't unfamiliar. I had already been taught that love was conditional, and that silence kept the peace. So when the abuse started, it didn't scream. It whispered. And I, still aching from a mother's absence and a sister's distance, believed him when he called it love. It didn't start with fists. It started with opinions—subtle critiques wrapped in concern.

"I don't like when you wear that."

"You shouldn't hang around her."

"You don't need to go to that dance—it's not for girls like you.

"He didn't raise his voice. He wrapped his control in softness, so it sounded like love. And I believed it—because no one had ever taught me that abuse can be quiet. I mistook domination for devotion, control for care. What I thought was protection was actually a prison with invisible bars. Slowly, piece by piece, he built a cage around my identity. At first, it felt like attention. He wanted to know where I was, who I talked to, what I wore. I convinced myself it meant I was special. That someone finally saw me. But over time, the questions turned to commands. The "I don't like that" became "You're not allowed." The "just checking in" became surveillance. And I complied—because love is supposed to compromise, right? But this wasn't compromise. It was submission. Not the kind that grows in a healthy relationship, but the kind that slowly steals your voice until you don't recognize your reflection.

He started a fight with me my senior year to try to make me miss homecoming. I was filled with so much pain, I missed birthdays. I missed being a teenager because he decided that freedom wasn't for me.

He wasn't protecting me—he was erasing me.

He started twisting my words behind my back. Sharing my secrets like gossip. Laughing at my pain in front of others to make me look unstable. Friends stopped calling. Family grew distant. Suddenly, I was too "dramatic," "too sensitive," "too much."

But I wasn't any of those things.

I was a girl who loved too hard, trusted too deep, and gave too much of herself to someone who only knew how to take.

He made me question everything—my feelings, my worth, even my sanity. Every time I cried, he'd say I was overreacting. Every time I pulled away, he'd guilt me with sweet words and shallow apologies. I began to doubt the very things I was experiencing. Was I imagining the pain? Was I being too emotional?

No.

I was being manipulated.

I wasn't too emotional—I was emotionally abused.

I wasn't imagining it—I was enduring it.

Abuse isn't always black and blue.

Sometimes it's slow.

Sometimes it's quiet.

Sometimes it's strategic.

But it's still abuse.

And when you finally have the courage to call it by its name, something begins to shift. You start reclaiming your power. Piece by piece, you gather the parts of you he tried to bury. You look in the mirror and say: "This isn't love. This isn't God's plan for me."

To anyone silently questioning their relationship, I say this:

Trust your gut.

If love feels like fear, like shrinking, like silence—**it's not love.** It's control. It's abuse.

And there is a God who sees you.

A God who is not in the business of shrinking you, but growing you.

A God who promises a hope and a future.

You were never meant to be small.

You were meant to rise.

* * *

.

Focus Scripture: Jeremiah 29:11 "For I know the plans I have for you," declares the Lord, "plans to prosper you and not to harm you, plans to give you hope and a future."

Journal Prompt: When did you first notice something didn't feel right? What signs were you taught to ignore?

Affirmation: I trust my instincts. I honor the warning signs I once silenced.

Chapter 6

The Physical Toll

My Body Remembered What My Heart Tried to Forget The first time he choked me, I saw darkness—not just from the lack of air, but from the shock that someone who claimed to love me could try to erase me. I blacked out. I woke up gasping, confused, unsure if it was real. He said I was exaggerating. That I was being dramatic. And I believed him. That's what abuse does it steals your clarity. The violence didn't stop there. He hit me while I was still recovering from a car accident he caused. He dragged me down the stairs while I was naked in front of his friend because he felt that I disrespected him. He didn't care who saw. He wanted to humiliate me, to break me from the inside out.

I learned to flinch before he even moved. My body was always tense. My laughter stopped and I stopped smiling as much. I felt dead inside and the scars from the car accident created a silence that reminded me every day that I was in prison, I would never escape from. My light dimmed. I wasn't just surviving the physical blows I was fighting the shame that came with them. And for years, I told no one how I felt inside, but everyone saw how he treated me on the outside.

Because how do you explain pain when you've been trained to protect the person who causes it? But my body knew. My nervous system remembered every hit, every threat, every silent scream. Trauma lived in my spine, in my skin, in my stillness. And now? My body is healing. I've given her permission to rest. I'm learning to feel safe again in my own skin, in my own home, in my own voice. I'm not ashamed anymore. I'm a survivor. And I'm standing in the full truth of what he did and what I overcame.

* * *

Focus Scripture Proverbs 3:5–6 – Trust in the Lord with all your heart and lean not on your own understanding; in all your ways submit to him, and he will make your paths straight.

Journal Prompt: How has your body carried your pain? What would your body say if it could speak?

Affirmation: My body is sacred. I am allowed to feel safe in my own skin.

Chapter 7

When Love Costs Everything

I had just received a $30,000 settlement. I thought, "Finally, we can breathe." I envisioned bills paid, a savings account, maybe even a fresh start for our family. But instead of using that money to build, he used it to destroy. He had no vision for stability—he had a fantasy. He wanted to be a kingpin. And he trusted the wrong people—one of whom turned out to be an informant. When everything fell apart and he got locked up, I was the one who wrote the statement to protect myself for once. But even then, I paid a price, a dangerous game. BUT I still stood beside him.

The same woman he betrayed, humiliated, and hurt. His best friend— his "brother"—wouldn't offer a dime. Told me to take out a loan. But instead, I took what I had and stood with him, I kept his name clean, kept the lights on, paid the car note because somewhere in me, I still hoped he'd become the man he pretended to be. Instead, he kept blaming me. Said I ruined him. But the truth is: he used me. He drained me emotionally, physically, and financially. I lost money, time, and peace behind his chaos.

Financial abuse is real. It doesn't just steal your wallet—it steals your security, your vision, your future. And even after

everything, he never offered a penny back. Never took account-
ability. But the money is gone, and I've rebuilt. What he tried to
take God restored. And this time, my investments are in peace,
purpose, and power. That's the wealth he can never steal again.

* * *

Focus Scripture: Isaiah 41:10 – So do not fear, for I am with
you; do not be dismayed, for I am your God

Journal Prompt: In what ways have you sacrificed your stability
or dreams for someone else? What do you need to reclaim financially or emotionally?

Affirmation: I am worthy of building a life rooted in peace, not
survival.

Chapter 8

Gaslighting and Lies

The Mind Games of a Narcissist
He lied with confidence. With a straight face. With charm that fooled everyone—except me. He told people I was cheating, unstable, unclean. That I was a liar. That I was crazy. And for a while, I started to believe it. That's what gas lighting does. It rewires your brain until you question your own memories.

He told me I was imagining things. That I was too emotional. That my reactions were the problem—not his actions. He accused me of cheating with friends from my past, and I wish I had. Maybe I did, in a moment, feel the need to be in love if it was only for one night or to feel that I was honorable to be loved, so if I did, I deserve too. But I didn't. I stayed loyal while he stepped out. Again, and again. And even after the betrayal, he spun a narrative that made him the victim and me the villain. He talked about me to every new woman. Especially to the woman he cheated with. Told her I was obsessed, broken, dangerous. But none of them knew the truth—the shotgun he pointed in my face. The slaps while I was healing.

The time he dragged me naked down the stairs. The way he gave out my business contacts just to ruin what I built. The messages I would read and never told a soul.

How he would say degrading things about me to other women he used to deal with and the late-night calls when he thought I was asleep and he would answer. The moments no one knows about and how he would cry to other women about how I hurt him and cheated, but little do they know he is the master of manipulation. He didn't just manipulate me—he manipulated everyone around me. Friends, family, even strangers.

He created chaos and made me look like the storm. But here's the truth: I'm not crazy. I'm not unstable. I was surviving a psychological war. And now? I'm free. To anyone who has ever been gaslight: You are not what they said. You are not what they made you feel. You are not the lies they told. You are the truth. You are light. And you are rising.

* * *

Romans 8:28 And we know that all things work together for the good to those who love God, to those who are called according to his purpose"

Journal Prompt: What lies where you told about yourself?What truths do you now believe about who you are?

Affirmation: I know who I am. No one can rewrite my truth but me.

Chapter 9

The Loss I Carried.
The Life I Gained.

For twelve years, I carried the desire to become a mother in the quietest, heaviest parts of my heart. We tried and tried, but nothing worked. Eventually, we sought the help of a fertility specialist, and the diagnosis came back as unexplained infertility. I thought he was the problem. But it was me. And he didn't support me through that truth—he let me carry that pain alone. I believed that if I gave him a child, he might love me better. Maybe he'd be softer. Maybe a baby would fix what was broken between us.

We went through two failed IUI rounds, and each one left me feeling more defeated. Then came the final round on our daughter's birthday, October 6. I was told to rest, stay calm, avoid stress. But peace wasn't something I could find in that house. That Sunday, I went through his phone—and found what I wasn't ready to see. He had been talking badly about me to another woman.

As he lay on the couch, I stared at his body and felt nothing but rage. Betrayal spilled out of me—I hit him, cried, screamed, and left. For two weeks, I stayed with my aunt, spiraling, stressed, smoking cigarettes, no longer caring about anything—not even the child I prayed for. That's when I realized: a baby was never going to fix a man who didn't want to be whole.

Then the test came back positive. I was pregnant. But when we went in for the third check-up, the heartbeat was gone. And deep down, I already knew why.

As I cried out in devastation, I saw a single tear fall from his eye. It didn't feel real. His pain looked like pride.

There was something in his smirk, his stillness—that told me he wasn't mourning with me. This wasn't just the loss of a child. This was the loss of hope. The loss of belief that love could come from him. No one truly understood the depth of my wounds. I sank into depression. Therapy became my lifeline. And slowly, I started to breathe again.

In 2019, God answered my prayers. He gave me the title I had begged for: Mother. I was overjoyed. But even in that moment, the one I needed to celebrate with me, refused. He wasn't happy not because of the child, but because of my joy. Because I had found something to love more than him. He began twisting stories. Telling people I had "secretly gotten a baby behind his back." But I didn't secretly get a baby behind his back, he knew that I had trouble conceiving a child, and a decision for her life had to be made quickly and I chose to be her primary care giver. I was heartbroken that he would treat me the way he did when I helped raise his daughter from the age of three. However I found out later that this was just another lie in the long line of narratives he used to make me look evil.

We were no longer husband and wife we were just two people coexisting under one roof. But the moment I laid eyes on my daughter, everything changed. I had purpose again. I had love again. I had a reason to rise. We were no longer husband and wife—we were just two people coexisting under one roof. But the moment I laid eyes on my daughter, everything changed. I had purpose again. I had love again. I had a reason to rise.

But then came September, the wedding. At our cousin's reception, I stood beside him while he walked across the room and flirted openly with a woman in the wedding party—laughing, smiling, and getting her phone number. He said it was for his cousin, but the disrespect was loud and clear. I saw through it. I felt the shame and the shift. I felt the dishonor. I remember vividly him sitting at my friends table like he was too comfortable, as I watch her pull his favorite liquor from the cabinet and serve him a beer, the knot in my throat wouldn't let me speak because all I can think of is how these events have unfolded right in front of me! Instantly the Holy Spirit shook me and opened my eyes. She was never a friend; she was on an assignment to destroy me as well. I know understood what it was like to have a Judas.

The betrayal ran deeper than I imagined. And when we left her house that day, He left our home and went straight to hers—his mistress. The woman who thought she was stealing something, when in reality, she was being used by God to release me. At the time, it felt like devastation. Like I was being replaced, humiliated, and tossed aside. I was still his wife legally, but no longer positioned in the role of his partner. I didn't see it clearly then but now I know: that woman wasn't my enemy. She was a blessing in disguise. She thought she was destroying me... but she was helping deliver me from the pit of hell I was too loyal to walk away from.

Sometimes God allows people to betray you so you can finally break free. She wasn't just the "other woman" she was a mirror that reflected just how far I had fallen from my worth. While she thought she had won a prize, what she actually did was confirm my exit. She took on the version of him that I had prayed would change. But God knew better. He knew I wouldn't leave until it hurt too much to stay. So, thank you. Thank you to the woman who thought she had one up on me. You didn't steal my man. You saved my life.

I cried the whole way home, driving with the pain of every sacrifice I had made. I remembered driving 13 hours to pick him up from Wisconsin. I remembered I had to put dreams on hold because he said NO! And now, what broke me most wasn't just that he moved on it was knowing he took everything I had taught him about how to love me as a woman and used it on someone else. He mimicked the love I had begged him to show me, not because he had changed, but because he knew how to perform now. He masked his true identity until he was sure he had her. And once she was hooked, the real him the man I had suffered under would eventually reveal himself to her too. I saw the screenshots and the post on social media.

Resemblance of things he did for me he began to do for her. He used the same bakery, the florist to love on her. He had went so far as buying things in two to give me one and her one. I remembered when he got dressed up in all white to go to a high school football game, he told me that lie but I knew he was going on a date with her. I didn't know at the time who she was, but I told him he looked nice and to have a great time, he smiled and left. I noticed her post on social media after I found out who she was, he took her to my favorite restaurant and ordered her my favorite drink. Now she was posting those things like they were hers—my favorite drink, my flowers, the restaurants I introduced him to, the gestures I longed for.

She wore my memories like new clothes, parading moments I helped create as if they were uniquely hers. And I just watched in silence, heartbroken and humiliated. That's when it hit me. I hadn't just lost a husband—I had lost myself. I lost the woman who used to laugh without second-guessing her worth. I lost the girl who believed love was supposed to feel safe. I lost the version of me who tried to shrink, mold, and break herself to make a man whole.

And in that moment, I realized: I had been grieving a marriage that had already buried me. But God didn't leave me there. Weeks passed and I cried out to God to let the healing began. He had been growing his locs for four years—through every season of our marriage, every high and every heartbreak. I had asked him many times to cut them, not out of control, but out of hope. A symbol. A reset. And every time, he said no.

But on the day the truth unraveled, the day God pulled back the veil and revealed the betrayal I had prayed to see clearly since 2018—he cut them. I had cried out for divine confirmation. I had begged God, "Show me what I need to see. Don't let me be blind to what's in front of me."

And that day, as I sat in my car, I heard the Holy Spirit say one word:

"Drive."

No directions. No names. Just that one command. So I drove.

And what I found shattered what little illusion I had left. The affair hadn't just begun—it had been festering for years, hidden beneath charm and control. But on October 1st, it all came to the surface. That was the day he cut his hair.

The same hair I once begged him to cut in the name of healing—he now cut in the shadow of shame. It was a ritual, a silent confession, a severing of everything we had built. I looked at the man I had loved for seventeen years...

And I didn't know him. His face was the same, but his spirit wasn't. His energy felt foreign. The love, the loyalty, the laughter we once shared—gone. That was the last scar he gave me. The final one that still stung. But that was also the day something shifted in me.

The day I let go.

The day I rose.

That was the day I began becoming the woman I was always meant to be. And the day he would remember for the rest of his life— not because he lost me, but because he watched me finally choose me.

Not whole yet, but healing.

Not finished, but free.

Not perfect, but no longer pretending.

That was the day I stopped fighting to be loved... and started fighting to be whole.

* * *

Focus Scripture: Ecclesiastes 3:4 – A time to weep, and a time to laugh; a time to mourn, and a time to dance.

Journal Prompt: Reflect on a time when your pain was invisible to others but all-consuming to you. What part of that experience have you yet to grieve fully and what would it look like to release it with grace?

Affirmation: I grieve with power. I heal with truth. I am no longer carrying shame for the pain someone else caused. God did not let it break me—He used it to build me. I am whole, even after the shattering.

Chapter 10

Loyalty Shouldn't Cost Your Soul

I stayed longer than I should have—not because I didn't see the signs, but because I believed that loyalty meant love. I thought that if I held on, remained faithful, and kept sacrificing, somehow things would turn around. I believed that love was proven through endurance.

But what I didn't realize was that I was staying loyal to someone who had already let go of me. Even when things were over between us, I continued to show up. I stepped in when you were struggling. I helped in ways no one knew about.

When your car was about to be repossessed and your image was on the line, I quietly paid the car note—not because I had to, but because I didn't want to see you fall. That's the kind of heart I have. I move in love, even when love hasn't been returned. I gave without asking.

I extended grace, even while I was hurting. And while I was doing all of this, you were speaking poorly of me, turning others against me, and keeping your hand closed when I needed help in return. I asked for support for our child—you said no. Still, I remained soft in a world that had hardened toward me.

But here's what I now understand: loyalty should never ask you to betray yourself. It should never require you to prove your worth through suffering. I confused resilience with love. I confused survival with connection.

Love should nourish, not deplete. Loyalty should lift, not burden. And now I know—real love starts with being loyal to me first. I will never again compromise my peace to protect someone else pride. And I will never again mistake sacrifice for partnership.

* * *

Romans 8:28 And we know that all things work together for the good to those who love God, to those who are called according to his purpose"

Journal Prompt: Think about a time when your loyalty caused you to neglect your own needs. What did you continue to give even when you weren't being supported? How can you begin to set boundaries that protect your peace without guilt?

Affirmation: I honor the love I gave, even when it wasn't returned. I no longer confuse self-sacrifice with loyalty. From now on, I choose me—with strength, grace, and peace.

Chapter 11

The Breaking Point

When Enough is Enough.
You betrayed me with someone who had no respect for herself, our relationship, or the family we were building. You left our family alone—not just physically, but mentally. I was unraveling, begging you to come home. And still, you rejected me. You turned your back on the woman who held you down when no one else would.

That day—when you looked me in the eye and said "no" that was the day I let go. I broke. But then I began to rebuild. I moved. Got my own place. Started over. You see, the breaking point wasn't just about you. It was about me. I realized I had been holding on to something that was draining the very life out of me. I had been loyal to a fantasy.

But God doesn't let us stay where we're not supposed to grow. And even after we divorced, you still tried to hurt me.

The choice that was made wasn't about starting over it was about striking a wound you knew existed. But healing took the sting out of your intentions. I stopped asking why. I stopped begging. I let go. And in that moment, I became free. I broke. But then I began to rebuild. And then God sent someone new—a man who was gentle with my broken pieces. A man who didn't flinch at my trauma or judge my scars. He didn't try to "fix" me. He held space for me. He prayed for me.

He loved me in silence and in presence. With him, I saw what love really looks like. A love that doesn't control. A love that doesn't compete. A love that sees you completely and doesn't run away from your healing.

* * *

Focus Scripture Psalm 147:3 – He heals the brokenhearted and binds up their wounds.

Journal Prompt: What was your breaking point? What moment made you choose yourself?

Affirmation: I let go with love. I rise with purpose.

Chapter 12

Healing is Not Linear

Some days I woke up strong. I cooked. I smiled. I breathed deep and felt the sun on my face like it was brand new. Other days, I couldn't get out of bed. I cried at stoplights. I questioned whether I really escaped or if I just traded one cage for another. That's the truth about healing—it's not a straight line. It's a winding, messy, raw road. And some days you'll take five steps forward and three steps back. But you keep going. That's what matters.

I struggled with guilt. I struggled with shame. I wrestled with memories that would sneak in out of nowhere—the sound of his voice, the smell of the house, the fear of being alone. Trauma doesn't just fade. It echoes. But healing? Healing is when you finally stop letting the echo drown your voice. I started going to therapy. I started praying for real again. I surrounded myself with women who didn't judge my pain, but sat with it.

And I stopped needing to explain why I stayed. I just started focusing on why I left. Every small decision I made to protect my peace was a declaration: I am worthy of love that doesn't hurt. I am worthy of safety. I am worthy of healing. Healing isn't about forgetting what happened. It's about choosing not to let it define you.

And now? I laugh again. I love again. I wake up and feel light in places that used to feel heavy. I'm not done healing—but I'm free.

* * *

Focus Scripture: Philippians 1:6 – He who began a good work in you will carry it on to completion.

Journal Prompt: What does healing look like for you to-day? Where do you still need grace for yourself?

Affirmation: Healing is a journey, not a destination. I am proud of how far I've come.

Chapter 13

You Are Not Alone And You Never Were

There were so many nights I thought I was the only one. The only woman walking on eggshells. The only mother hiding bruises beneath makeup and smiles. The only soul quietly begging God to let her survive just one more day. But I wasn't alone—and neither are you. Abuse is isolating by design. It convinces you no one would believe you. That your story is too messy. That your trauma is too deep. That you're too damaged. But that's a lie. The truth is: there are millions of us. Warriors. Survivors.

Queens who made it through hell with their crowns still tilted high. You are not weak for staying. You are not crazy for loving. You are not broken for believing. You are human. And you are stronger than you think. There are women out here who will listen. Women who won't judge.

Women who will nod their heads as you speak because they've lived it too. This book? This is my hand reaching for yours. My truth linking arms with yours. A reminder that what you lived through was real—and so is your healing. If you're reading this, let me speak directly to your spirit:

You are not alone.

You were never alone.

There is a community of love, faith, sisterhood, and truth waiting to receive you. You belong to something greater than your pain.

You are seen.

You are heard.

And you are worthy of peace.

* * *

Focus Scripture: Deuteronomy 31:6 – Be strong and courageous. Do not be afraid or terrified because of them, for the Lord your God goes with you.

Journal Prompt: Who in your life supports your healing journey? Who do you need to thank or release?

Affirmation: I am surrounded by love, support, and sisterhood. I am never alone.

Chapter 14

Redemption-Love That Looks Like God

After all the trauma, loss, betrayal, and heartbreak—I never expected to find love again. Not real love. Not the kind that restores you. But God had a plan far greater than my pain. And when

He sent my true husband into my life, I knew... this was different.

He didn't come into my world trying to fix me.

He came ready to cover me.

To cherish me.

To know me.

He saw the broken places and didn't flinch.

He held space for my healing.

He was gentle with my scars, not ashamed of them—but in awe of the strength they proved. He became my safe place. My calm. My partner. My Husband. My King. Together, we moved to a new state. A new beginning. We started building—businesses, ministry, family. Not just dreams, but legacy. The same God who once held me through loss has now gifted me with abundant restoration. He provides for our family with excellence.

He loves me with patience. He supports me in purpose. We have launched a marriage ministry, planted a church, and co-lead from a place of humility, love, and laughter. He embodies Ephesians 5—not just in words, but in action.

In him, I found a man who doesn't compete with my strength, but compliments it. A man who holds me close, prays over me, and reminds me daily that love was never supposed to hurt the way I once thought it did.

My husband contributes to me being a better woman.

A better wife. A better mother.

A better daughter.
He loves the version of me that others tried to destroy and because of that, I continue to rise.

This is redemption.

Not perfect.

But real.

Not fantasy. But favor. And it is more than I ever imagined.

* * *

Focus Scripture: Ephesians 5:25 – Husbands, love your wives, just as Christ loved the church and gave himself up for her.

Journal Prompt – Think about what love looks like to you now. After everything you've been through, what does healthy feel like in your body, your spirit, and your mind?

How has God shown you that redemption is not just possible— but promised?

Affirmation: I am not just a survivor. I am redeemed. I am loved without fear, held without conditions, and supported without limits. My scars do not define me—they remind me that I was made for more. God didn't just bring me through... He gave me better.

Chapter 15

Your Turn to Let Go

ALetter You'll Write One Day
One day, you'll sit down like I did. Maybe with a pen. Maybe with a laptop. Maybe with tears streaming down your face. And you'll start writing—not to them, but to yourself. You'll write your way out of the shame.

Out of the silence. Out of the storm. It won't be pretty at first. It may come out angry. Raw. Grief filled. You may not even know what you're trying to say. But as the words pour out, so will the weight. And with every sentence, you'll feel yourself exhale for the first time in a long time. You'll write about the nights you almost gave up. The days you begged for love in return for pain.

The moments you thought you'd never be whole again. And then, you'll write about how you survived. How you stood back up. How you remembered who you were before they convinced you were nothing. Letting go doesn't mean pretending it didn't happen. It means finally deciding it doesn't control you anymore. It means releasing the anger, the fantasy, the need for closure. It means saying: "I've carried this long enough. Now I choose me."

This chapter is yours now.

You've lived through what tried to destroy you.

And you are still here.

Now breathe.

Stand tall.

Walk in the light.

Because letting go?

That's how you rise.

* * *

Focus Scripture: Revelation 21:4 – He will wipe every tear from their eyes. There will be no more death or mourning or crying or pain.

Journal Prompt: Write your own "letting go" letter. Address it to the person, pain, or version of yourself that no longer serves you.

Affirmation: Letting go is not a weakness—it is the beginning of my freedom.

About the Author

Quansheeba L. Long is a devoted mother, wife, daughter, a passionate educator, and a bold advocate for women and children impacted by domestic violence. With a Master's degree in Education, she has dedicated her life to nurturing and empowering others—both in the classroom and throughout her community.

She is the co-founder of QCK Photography, a creative venture she shares with her husband, and the visionary leader behind Leading Ladies of NC, a nonprofit organization that uplifts women through ministry, mentorship, business support, and life empowerment.

Quansheeba also founded EmpowerHer, a youth program for girls ages 7–12 focused on building self-worth, mental wellness, and life skills.

An ordained Minister of the Gospel, she and her husband, Pastor Quentin S. Long, faithfully serve through their online ministry, The House of Hope Inc., where they are committed to reaching souls and restoring hearts through Christ.

Quansheeba is also the host of the powerful podcast Painfully Purposed, available on Spotify, where she shares her journey and encourages others to rise from their own valleys with faith and strength.

A proud member of Sigma Gamma Rho Sorority, Inc., she is committed to service, sisterhood, and uplifting her community.

She currently resides in the beautiful state of Texas, where she continues to live out her calling to inspire, lead, and love.